MW00386676

This Journal Belongs To:

______________________________